MW01519569

Light-crossing

Also by Michael Redhill

Poetry
Music for Silence
Impromptu Feats of Balance
Lake Nora Arms
Asphodel

Fiction
Martin Sloane

Drama
Building Jerusalem

As Editor
A Discord of Flags (with Steven Heighton and Peter Ormshaw)
Blues & True Concussions: Six New Toronto Poets
Lost Classics (with Michael Ondaatje, Esta Spalding, and Linda Spalding)

.ight-crossing   Michael **Redhill**   poems

Anansi

Copyright © 2001 Michael Redhill

All rights reserved. No part of this publication may be reproduced or transmitted in any form or by any means, electronic or mechanical, including photocopying, recording, or any information storage and retrieval system, without permission in writing from the publisher.

Published in 2001 in Canada and in 2002 in the United States by House of Anansi Press Limited 895 Don Mills Road 400-2 Park Centre Toronto, ON M3C 1W3 Tel. 416-445-3333 Fax 416-445-5967

Distributed in Canada by General Distribution Services Ltd. 325 Humber College Blvd. Etobicoke, ON M9W 7C3 Tel. 416-213-1919 Fax 416-213-1917 E-mail cservice@genpub.com

Distributed in the United States by General Distribution Services Inc. PMB 128, 4500 Witmer Industrial Estates Niagara Falls, NY 14305-1386 Toll Free Tel. 1-800-805-1083 Toll Free Fax 1-800-481-6207 E-mail gdsinc@genpub.com

www.anansi.ca

05 04 03 02 01   2 3 4 5

CANADIAN CATALOGUING IN PUBLICATION DATA

Redhill, Michael, 1966–
Light-crossing

Poems.

ISBN 0-88784-657-2

I. Title.

PS8585.E3425L53 2001   C811'.54   C00-933186-7
PR9199.3.E42L53 2001

Cover design: Angel Guerra   Typesetting: Brian Panhuyzen
Printed and bound in Canada

THE CANADA COUNCIL | LE CONSEIL DES ARTS
FOR THE ARTS | DU CANADA
SINCE 1957 | DEPUIS 1957

We acknowledge for their financial support of our publishing program the Canada Council for the Arts, the Ontario Arts Council, and the Government of Canada through the Book Publishing Industry Development Program (BPIDP).

Contents

III

I found you with this . . .
— Buddy Guy

Anne,

I

Gods

The gorse-edged trail, the path up through sheep laurel and sedge
by the lake, and then up again through the meadow and remnants
of orchard and mill. Nine-months pregnant, you leaned back
into shadow under a russet-thick apple tree, then on after that
to the edge of the pine forest, the signs promising
a circle back to the parking lot. Still later, a steel bridge brought us
over the river, the water bursting against the mesh-encased blocks
buttressing the tracks that once went to Waterford and Kitchener,
and here there was another road and we were lost. We'd arrived this way
in another summer, and gone down to water. I remembered that time —
I didn't know if I loved, or was loved, but now that felt like the past.

Climbing to the road, gleaming and ravenous, you fell into a café chair,
I went back for the car. Over the river, the bridge, ancestral memory
of a train going past, a hint of doubt, then forest, then meadow, running
because the baby could come at any time. Then orchard and mill, and why
did I stop to look at the old stones, the dead shapes close
to the ground saying something about what they'd been used for? Why
did I lie down where you had, now the sky different, the light different? Although

the flowing reek of apples was the same, the flattened shape
in the grass. It was as if that old other part of my life was over,
and I was here to remember it, the way we'd been. Like that dead family
who ground grain here and fed carrots to the horses, and turned
that great wheel we thought probably fit into a groove in the side
of one of the crushed walls, and baked, and made love, and there was
no city below them, and nothing above them but the sky and its gods.

December 1998

Dishonest

Floating along the edge of a party, hearing
the stories you are a part of. All of it resists you.
Or you resist it. It's not clear anymore. A light
in the backyard seeps down; it's a streetlamp
behind a tree. The shadow inside the branches
looks like a hanging man. Now, this is a story
you could tell, but you don't. Something
you are afraid of, that stalks you
every minute of your life. So
return to the party and be among friends.
Tell a story, your back to the window.

Reconciliation

For two hours they've argued, their language strange,
their predicament familiar. Late-hour tea-drinkers,
all of us silent at our tables, take sides. He's
vivid, his hands holding her in his angry
atmosphere, yet
I want him to win, want her to take him back as much
as the café's women want to move to the young girl,
their bodies bent into her as if she were light.
She's dressed in black, steadied at the table
with her hands splayed, her back taut, her legs
braced under the table as if for aftershocks. To his
pleas — so busy-mouthed, so darting-eyed — she offers
birdlike demurrals. Across the room a woman sits alone,
hands cupped around the heat of a mug and I want
to go to her suddenly, kiss her hands, her mouth, but don't,
am locked to the vision of his fingertips leaving
white aureoles on her arm. How long before she breaks?
Her head goes down and she shudders,
he puts his hand in her black hair. *Mi corazón*, she says
and kisses him over the empty plates.
I can see her eyes behind her shaking lids

the pupils so nervous and sexual under
the pale skin that I could be watching her sleep,
seeing her face in the deepest part of the night
when your lover dreams and you cannot wake her.

Comfort

A dating doxology: the night
barely on and already the fresh couple
talking god. She says, *comfort me*, and he
pours wine but she means *get closer*.
All night the different bells in their heads,
the round seeds in their bodies
like marbles in a hand. How many ways
a hand can close: in another hand, around itself,
in the grasp of a sad thing too soon said.
Love is . . . he'd like to say and know
what she wants to hear, but laughs
the thought off. A head inclines
as if to pray, but really
it's only one of them
putting on a coat.

The Night

The day was spent in rain. Trucks
slid into the curbs, shook
when their engines were turned off.
I was wearing what I wore
when we first met. Someone
spoke your name and I
took off my glasses, cleaned them
quietly. In another life,
I am tending children, we
make love under trees. Today
I walked the streets and gazed at women
shopping in windows. Their hands
grazed over shirts on hangers,
languid faces, their long fingers slow
over the empty bodies. You once stood crying
on my porch after the long walk home.
A year later I moved from that house. Now
I live with my sins.

The Lost River

I
The streets and gardens
have closed over it, a wire
vanishing into a tree. The Iroquois
had a name for it, but I don't know that name
now, only know its underground path
from the willow near your house.
After a cold, heavy rain it can seep up
like blood through a bandage,
leaking into the street. The lost river
wants to find its old shores. But mostly
we encounter its ghost: an imprint
left in a bellied curve scooped out of the park,
tombstones crowning its head
near the airport cloverleaf.

II
The body does not continue,
but buries itself in flesh. Old cuts
burrow, lie like arrowheads
under skin. There's a silky
patch over your knee where a nail went in.
Its narrow iron puncture spread
to a stop-motion ripple —
picture of a fish leaping, stilled.
Our own thin tributaries
bear healing up, carry off decay, leave
their whorls and furrows. A blue
translucence stays
on the surface.

III

At Harrison Street, we're standing
under the pale willow, the mourner
who won't leave the graveside. Under here,
its roots reach down, bring a dead voice
green into the air. We draw water, sit in the bath.
What washes off us drains to where the river
remembers our secret life: there, a willow
grows from my wrist, your hand
tips into the lake and the water flows
down your arm and through your fingers. The river
had a name for us, but we don't know that name
now. Our bodies in the bed sculpt the hollow
the river left in the park.

Commodore Jarvis

Lakes too, bearing up the clumsy steamers,
cheap galleons filled with lumber, fish, wood
for caskets. 1875. The city seeped forward — this July
they found the Commodore Jarvis rotting under the expressway
tore up its ash and dust for the new stadium. Its last trip,
it put in at the Yonge Street pier, unloaded
apples from New York state, trout from Vermont.
Then they invented basketball. Mackenzie King
went for control of the city's new electrics.
Charlie Conacher and Busher Jackson walked up Church
in their overcoats, lost to Detroit, walked home.
After a few years, radios started to get smaller,
they tore down the tall red trade centre
at Front and Yonge. My grandfather was born
across the ocean and they named him Israel. That same year
a boy from Corktown fell through the ice
playing hockey on Lake Ontario. He lies there now,
undiscovered, or else
beneath a downtown hotel. Preserved
like a silvered bog man, his skin

tight across his bones, his ribs
rounded under the leather coat like
streetcar tracks mounded with snow.

Yonge Street Is Two Hundred Years Old Today

and you can ride the Dianetics elephant
at St. Mary Street free (fifteen seconds per load,
a thirty second pause for hay refuel
and then it's led around
with a metal claw) or you can just send
your kid into the Conklin Moon Walk,
its yellow and red vinyl sluiced
with misty rain. In 1855 it cost
one cent for every pig in your cart
to pass south of Bloor; today there's
veggie dogs. There was grass here, too
(the other kind), and small
insurrections witnessed by housewives
from their Jarvis Street windows.
Today, the Pilot Tavern street buffet
is empty (capacity one thousand)
and sloth-eyed little girls drip pizza oil
onto their frocks, a word
not much used anymore. This
was all orchards, my grandfather told me.
Apple trees with their black twisted limbs

against hills and Indian sky. Today, there's a man
holding his arm high in the air
empty hand cupped, plucking at nothing.
At the middle of Yonge and Bloor.

College & Montrose

Elsewhere, the city fathers
debate where to put the bridges —

and my mother, in a yellow slicker,
walks up College Street, crosses
in the skin-warm air
to the movies.

On her neighbour's lawn
an electron fires and a peach-blossom
opens.

It rains at four o'clock, but my mother,
as a young girl, is inside the cinema

where a woman cries for help
beneath the swinging
silver blade. Then the lights come on.

My grandfather, still quick in his grey suit,
meets her, they walk to the bakery
near Montrose. They cross the buried river

that every living thing
drinks from, that runs
in their bodies — once

there, once on the way home,
my mother waiting while he buys the rye,
the narrow railings inside
scare her, and the fact that her father
holds a number while he waits.

She stands squinting in the May sun, turning
a red wooden ball in her hands.

Then they go home with the bread
hot as a baby in swaddling. After, there are
the moves, the marriage and children, death,
the bakery and cinema gone, no photos.
But the peach tree. The river. This window
that looks out on it.

Sudden

I

Black and yellow, a sepiaed X ray, the edge and centre of a bruise. Shallow
water at the lake-rim is yellow, looking down from a canoe (the distant
chirring of a chipping sparrow, cicada in birch, the whonk of beavertail)
the water is black, bracken and mud closed to the sky's wingfilled blue. Sharp
Halloween colours, bringing memory of Toronto fall, yellow leaves, wirey
air. But here, anaphylaxis, honey-gold venom and my mother dead at fifty-six.

II

Or rescued, the luck of a smalltown ambulance trundling past, the attendants
eating popcorn in the front seat out of their oil-grimed hands, the radio
alive with bad news. She's alabaster pale, her own death tribute, coldsweat
and hivey red on the table, her stomach war-mapped with red dots showing
the enemy positions. Ministrations: cuff and cold disk, a sting for blood, the old
nurse's lessons coming back as she diminishes, every cell shrunk in stark refusal
and back at the lake, the ice cubes are melting slowly in her drink.

III
A few weeks later, Benjamin discovers birds. Lying flat on my chest he follows
the pale grey-and-white shapes crossing the sky. Sham unity comes apart:
everything moves independent, is separate, things can disappear. Near us, nectar-drunk
bumblebees lumber from one flower to the next, airborn bison, a mistake
that works. Somehow, they get home and deep in those nests the sugar cures
to thickness and is never suspect although it can kill a child. There is a trace of poison
in pleasure. With those new teeth, he bites when he kisses.

IV
Hysteria parts the traffic, manic lights flashing the siren raw as a voice saying
it's you, it's you, it's you, it's her, gas-masked and resurfacing. My father
follows behind, rational as math, papering hornetlike round and round
the claw-filled panic. But she lives, she lives, and her birthday will come again
and there will be cake and the childhood wax-scent of candles, and later,
the morbid puns: *venom I ever going to hear the end of this I-almost-died story?*
But not thoughts of *nearly* nor the extra minute somehow not wasted nor
all of us in the city, happily ignorant, nor her, black-humoured saying
today you would have buried me.

v

From a maze of others, out of the cramped dark, you came looking for quiet
and solace in the dozey heat. Black and yellow like a bruise, a memory of the fall,
or the striped corduroy turtlenecks she once dressed me in: she didn't know
better, neither did you, settling in the cool dark of a pantleg. But this is
not an elegy, tiny power, not for you, although after this, everything is forgiven,
you are forgiven, you with your accidental death clenched in you like a shout.
Spent and empty you became weightless and sudden in a hand and we read your name
in the field guide, *yellowjacket*, and this was the last thing said of you. Back home,
you weren't missed, although you died for your mother, who made you, and now goes on.

July 1999

Gladioli

The glads won't open with their points against the window —
your dying friend told us this, then asked you
to get her husband on the phone. (He's bone
and hair now, starwatching under ten winters.) It was
only the end of summer, but beginning to feel like fall,
the hospital wildflower garden a plot of stalks.
In the parking lot, a man walked his wife in her chair
through the light and dark, sun and shadow, seasons.
His hat in her lap like a brown dog curled up,
so ridiculous in her thinness, her death's script
coming out of her mouth — that wasn't her, I knew
she would never say those things. We greeted
the man in the lot and his wife, civil, all of us
civil about the whole thing, and then we drove north
where hotter weather was promised. Now it's so dark out
I can't tell where the trees end and the sky begins, that long
dark commensurate with time. But I can't open my eyes now,
my face pressed against the window.

Distant

Silent house tonight, the dog at the in-laws' and you on the coast,
and outside the distant revellers from the losing team have taken
so forlornly to the streets. It's weeks before the baby arrives
and a whole year until the lost one, and are these the last
peaceful hours of the old life? Once I walked home in the dead hours,
a lover dozing in her bed behind me, and you still in another city,
our lives years of connections apart. And in the streets that night,
all the defeated lovers were trudging back to their
bachelor lairs, shoulders hunched in the wind, the smell of someone they now forget
on their wrists. Tonight I've listened to the stray gongs
and drumbeats below and know these are the sounds of wondering
what to hope for next. What did I want before now? How
did I put it to myself, bewildered about everything except that
I did not love that woman? Only I loved the cold aura of the night
and the other men in it, and felt sad for being apart from you
some time in the future.

August 1998, October 1999

Night Driving

Dark villages, asleep for hours now, sweep by, candles flickering in windows.
I go through Main Street, Magellan under the moon, the gas station shut
until morning, the road muffled in snow. Trumansburg, Covert, Ovid.
Silent towns. I'm a shooting star, the night lit up
through the windshield. In the washed-out skies of my childhood,
sometimes a dim star would urge itself over the rooftops, or we'd go
to the planetarium and gape at the universe in a bowl. But here's the true
starblown night, scattered salt thrown for good luck over a shoulder.
Passing by wintering fields, the cupolaed farmhouses wheel past
cloaked in faint light, their basements reliquaries of war, bones
and scuppered backhoes lying under the plowed corn. I pull over, blind
from my own lights cupping snow into the fading distance.
Standing at a lookout over dark Cayuga, the long lake
seems a tear in the world, my world with stars at its centre.

April 2000

Mahoney Point

Green-backed and humped the hills
slope there like mossed wheels
turning slow out of the water and the water
green itself like a memory of those hills.
Somewhere in the distance
you showed us the gap to the giant sea,
the buoys with their safe-home instructions.
Industry threw up a few good bridges, too —
a lock that turns. Although gas puddles
near the waterline. That immense green
soothes itself, thighs and bellies of earth
moving under the sun so slow
our lifetimes in these small bodies
won't measure it. Reminders of this
in the white steeples tossed
onto the hills. At night
someone inside the trailer
throws their cards down *splat*
in disgust and dislodged bats arrow into the light
creaking and clicking, their pinhole eyes
flashing like beetles. If you stand alone
in a wet field under stars you find out

how few words there are for things —
even the night is trying to put it all into a poem.
But the Milky Way is a chalk mark
erased against blackness.

Allen's Hill

Remember the swallows, the wrens
twisting into light like novas? An iron thresher
was buried in weed near the dark mouth
of the barn, a black underpass
where the machinery once went. Meanwhile,

the civil war dead
leaned up into light
on the hill behind, their white crosses
tick-marks on a page, softened by rain:
stone fleurs de lys. We'd driven for hours,

wanted to see rivers and waterfalls.
The huge gorge nearby
was empty, logs lay in it
like twigs. Everything reeked of accident there:
Pennsylvania beer
served between cornfields, county roads
that met by chance in swipes of dust.

That night a man told us his life
and a house up the road

were the same thing. We wanted
to belong to the world that way.
While we slept that night

more weeds grew over the foundations
of a Shaker house hidden in the woods.
Closer, the barn breathed the night air.
The moon shone in the cracks, lit
the eyes of dormice, cats, and owls:
wild starlight.

Seam

Tender to think how others cling to your goodness,
when what you are browns out from time to time and leaves you less,
but in this bad light you look the same, are loved anyway. Worse,
there are so many books you've forgotten, and also the few
names of trees and childhood ravines. And when your loved ones
are away, you long for them as if they were dead, but when together,
you want to be alone. Suddenly, it appears the old contradictions
are not going to be resolved, they've settled, bound forever,
for good. No scarper to disguise it will work, the blemish
looks more like you every hour. We live speaking hopefully
of the goodness in others, wanting to lose that stymied wish
to give love. You think it's buried in childhood's grey quarries.
But if that's true, the future is more cold. Better to want less.
And make no more poems until you are old.

II

Heat Wave I

The girl suspended in peach liqueur. A man
walks arms splayed. The watery air
is road anklet, the weft at foot level,
water-fire. The cafés are fogged and still,
couples sitting like heads on spikes
hovering over sweating waterglasses. Metal
is nervous, perspires at the gangster onslaught,
lovers will say anything, slurred,
in salt drunkenness: *blow on me*. The day stands too close,
cars slowly drive by, the neighbourhood's
microwave magnifying, decking
old women, men with metal sewed in
under their skins. In the evening, the glassy-eyed
weatherman wipes his face, and the city's fattest men
lie in bed with fans in their armpits, apartments
release their tenants to city greens,
women in loose tanks, men in underwear —
a return to roots, life in the trees, in forests
carved out by rivers and glaciers
somewhere in a gelid past.

Heat Wave II

Pero, al sólo ver a está mujer
se me olvida tojo
                    — *Pablo Neruda*

At the mere sight of this woman
I forget everything else. I forget
poetry and its balms, I forget
love's absence, the unclimbed stairs.
I can't recall the way doors
open in my house, lose track
of my halls, which, unsupervised,
race out into the open air. My guests
sit unserved in the front room,
my friends leave after knocking.

Have pity on me. I walk out at night
and the heat-stricken sunflowers
raise their heads to show me
their thousand-kissed faces.
I fear love's arrival,

but if love comes for me
I will raise my heat-stricken head
to be kissed. I will open my doors and lay down
red runners along my hallways. I will
keep soup on my stove, bring air
into my rooms, and sleep on the floor.
I will happily forget my life if love
comes for me. If love remembers me.

Heat Wave   III

Strange wire-thin heat
the bar's copper-green head of Zeus
drips a wax crown
and a girl's perm comes undone.
Sweating, you gorge on tangerine,
tug at seams to Venus your shirt,
take these arms up
against the advancing warmth, heat
like stealth. When I saw you
step off the curb this morning,
your white shirt buzzed green
behind my eye. You
were the only person
I could have touched today.

Heat Wave IV

Primordial snooze, sleep a Catherine wheel
and nighttime apartments convect.
The green heartshaped leaves nod
as if ethered, send tendrils
down to the cool floor. You
sweep by on your bike, raise a hand —
hello to me and surrender to the day.
Your black hair off your neck coiled
high, oncoming night's relief
holds the same promise: the dark falling
at last.

Heat Wave v

The green water bottles build up by the door,
a meadow of glass cool as an insect eye.
You're waiting at the bottom of the stairs,
your body boxed by the fragmented windows.
Come up, come up — *slowly* I think. I watch your knees
slipping in and out of your short pants.
Now, arpeggio of water filling a glass,
hopefulness that you'll stay a while,
endure this heat in your white cotton shirt.
What can be done? About this other person
who loves you? I want to commit a crime!
Every inch of air inspires flesh
when we move into it.
I instruct my desire to unhand me. I
would like to be sensible for once.
But you put your glass down,
move your hair over an ear, and I see
skin there. As I suspected.

Heat Wave VI

The city under rain, the long streets
gleaming black with freshets, braids
of water spinning into the sewers. You
spread out on the bed, the sweat on your back
perfect saltpools magnifying. Your hands
flow over the sides. (The night after this, I came home
in another storm, saw the windows open
to rain. The bed was soaked black as the streets,
the sky surging in the window.)

Heat Wave VII

Let's get together and finish
what we haven't started. My body's
about to bolt and go to seed. I might turn into
Ezra Pound in a cage without you, without you
I'll sit in these paved places forever
and watch crushed coffee lids skitter
like sparrows. What happened here
that I remember once
so green and touchable? Is the body
really as lush as the earth?

Heat Wave VIII

Summer ends in a wave of rain seen
over milky coffee: café
meteorology. Over the trees on Clinton
a patch of blue retreats, goes grey,
goes black, bursts, and in the streets nipples appear
like secret code revealed. People walk calm
through the white downpour, their mouths pinched,
others run, flatfooted tsunamis flashing up.
A cowering dog is collar-hauled by its soaking owner
down through the running day. Just hours ago,
you agreed to meet me by the buses. *Let's go,*
you said. *The day is open.*

Creaturely

A snarl of words
tails out like rust in water,
goes to clear, emptiness
of the mouth
before sudden lovemaking.
Animal time,
                    so we, creaturely,
surrender, watch the clean motion
a little fearful, see
the way our bodies
                    want us. Then, forgetting,
we murmur bliss, this
clamour this danger of flesh,
deathful and hungry.
We say *love*
but the word is just
the remains
at well-bottom,
                    nothing added
to the rivetting zero,
a teleology, a condition,
                    a gene.

Cold Snap I

Such a long summer — it went on
until fall came like a breath
being let out. I myself
turned blue from being alone, all
that heat and nothingness,
turning around in bed
like it was an ocean. I dreamt of you,
and of you, the hair of one,
the breasts of another. Love
assembled its carnage all summer long.
Now the rain is falling, the relief
of honesty, it's about time
someone said what they were feeling
around here. So cold outside —
November on its way, with its charms
of sciatica, blackened leaves in the gutters,
dogs shivering in argyle sweaters.

Cold Snap II

Pathetic fallacy, she noted, the trees
limp with ice. I was too tired, to be
honest. For weeks it felt like that,
the walls shadowy with clumps of snow,
the slow falling, the stillness of the streets.
The quintet of windows across the way
filled with blue light every evening,
the sprawling reflection of a cop show
flicked lazily on a wall. The fire in our grate
picked up the paint job, lit up the underblue
like the memory of a pond. And at the edge of it,
the flame shadowed reverse fireflies, like the snow
falling on the wall in the bedroom.
There was some cold in us as well, but
you threw your good shadow across that too.

Cold Snap III

The night of Remembrance Day,
you slept with the dog sighing on your chest.
I was sitting at the kitchen table
and the dim light from the Y lay across my arms
like a shawl. For all time,
I want to remember these things —
your breath soughing in the bedroom,
the rumble from the dog's throat,
the glass tabletop against
the warmth of my arm.
I want all this to last.

Cold Snap IV

Liebefurcht

First snowfall, terror of death.
At dinner, friends laughed over a game
then stood at the top of the stairs,
as though grief had come. I walked home
with someone I didn't know,
whose mistakes were invisible,
who, I'm sure, believed things
anathema to me. When we walked by
the gin palaces on Sherbourne,
voices roared out of doors.
Knowing about sex in the hollowed rooms
of the Leonard Hotel embarrassed us.
She told of a friend
who had fallen in love and married
in six days. I felt afraid of that.
We walked a few blocks more,
performed the oblations of strangers.
On the streetcar a memory of you
ambushed me from the afternoon.

Cold Snap v

The migrators come back, squat
in the park in their green and
brown glory and look querulous;
is this squelch and muck the end
of renewal's flight path? No world
but ours thaws so slowly: a woman holding
a stiffly weeping man. Spring's firstborn robin
edges onto the nest-rim, then plunges
drenched and frozen to the frosted lawn.

Cold Snap VI

Grateful now
for the lengthening days,
the fall of light, the purpled evening
deep inside our rooms
the weather of our bodies.
"Our first winter" — dozing
in the cooling room, these words
test themselves. How many more
late nights will we be allowed
to hear the wind whistling
between the houses? Winter is not
such a poor time to love someone.
I can hardly believe the myriad things
clenched in stillness underground
as you lift the covers to your bed.

Any Day Now

Music saves me. From passing cars, the brief
swell of a radio, someone else's distraction
on the way to work. Imagine that life, arrowing off
to another place and then another, that music
pulled with it. So it is with us, the bits of song
that attach to times, fabric torn away on the barb.
For me, always the amateur, I can't even remember
the names of songs, but the urgencies return, the stretch
in Nina Simone's voice singing *I shall be released*,
the unaccountable grief unleashed by *I still have
that other girl in my head.* Injected like ink under skin,
broken-off wish-songs, talisman drum breaks, long fades.

Translucent

Mediums of light, venetian blinds casting ribbons
of morning across the bed, dust in its armies marching down,
your skin glowing in sleep. Light has weight, the sun
annexing leaves and bodies, it inhabits the skin's phosphor.
I remember the pink radiance of a penlight against a hand, or tucked
in a cheek, the blood carrying light, the cool black at the middle of flesh
where it couldn't go. The seeming solidity of our bodies, a necessary
faith, thinking we can't be bent by mirrors, altered by lenses,
believing ourselves bone-substantial. I've held
my son in fever and felt his head, heavy with light. Born, he burst gold,
the last stage of sun and leaves and these light-crossing bodies. Before us,
an illumination, after us, a glow. I reach around you,
open the blinds and cover your eyes against the morning.

Bridge to Benmiller

The old supports are gone, along
with the waterfall that had flowed under it, only
the grey concrete pylons holding an empty pose
between the banks, men in black suits walking
in mid-air. Over the ice and cold January sluice
the new concrete bridge spans, the road
is straighter. Near here, the burying grounds
of the Attawandaron, who guarded flint, were friends
to warring nations. Gone, and their cemeteries
wooded over: new cedar, new birch, vertical canoes
returned to source, marking their graves. Hear
the syncopated clack and whirr, the looms, the mills,
the giant wheels for the river turbines. Some of it
suburban fixtures now. Industry in trees. I can see
the bridge to Benmiller from the window,
the Sunday paper fanned out along the floor
and you asleep, winter sunlight a yellow balm
over the blanket.

Cependant

In the traces of creosote from the neighbour's walls, a memory, not mine
of the settlers' smoky outbuildings, the black tar seeping into the green
where later the vested conquerors played golf. One had massed his troops
too far east, guarding the mouth of the river, the other climbed the cliffs
with the future in his teeth. This morning, the song of finch and grackle
weave the air, two languages, and the neighbour's new basement yields
pottery fragments where he crushes his cigarettes (wondering
what grainy soups were once spooned up from it). The book in front of me forces
caincailleries and *cependant* up through the yellow air but I forget words
as soon as I learn them, stumble back onto standbys, communicate
without expressing. In the old city, foreign brides are defrocked *en masse*, later
they stand under the statues squinting in the river-reflected light. Walking
through the plains later, I see groundhog whelps nested in a cup of
red fabric, their blind heads searching through the gold thread for milk.

Sugar

Cutting through bands of brown and grey, fields still fallow
even though it's June, my thirty-third birthday
passing on a train to Montreal. Seed lying in furrows, long lines
cut into the distance, spin to pointed spokes at the window,
the rest of it fanning out like the pages of a book
falling open. At the edge of scabby oak and silver maple, the white
apiary boxes tilt against each other, sodden with honey, and I'm
coming back to you, to our rooms and our lives, sweet
accretions of another language seeping through me. From the train
it's mostly the near view: green arbour blurring past and small lanes
in the copses appearing and vanishing with their vistas of cirrus and river
behind, and the lake flat in the distance, blue monolith. Last night
I danced until the beau monde sagged around me, shriven of the hunger
that brought us there. With time, that hunger ambers to heavy —
it slows and directs us, a summer ripening. Laden with a new year, our lives
various within us, I am honing in to you.

On the day you were born

for Kougar Singh

Outside, everything continued
as if nothing important was happening.
The first pictures of a plane wreck were coming in.
A fat man in the doughnut shop was eating salty pieces of celery
out of a plastic container. In the evening I was beaten in Scrabble,
and earlier, the night had become cold. My mother and I
sat in a car instead of having a walk. She said,
I'm at an age where I know when I'm myself and when I'm not.
We agreed love and sadness are the two things all people submit to.
I say to those things, *Take me*. Looking at new life,
we coo for what it doesn't know yet. Love I don't have to explain.
I stood with your father outside. He was ten thousand eight hundred
and forty-three days old. We were waiting across the road from the hospital,
as if the most beautiful thing could also frighten us.
Your mother lay in that room with you, ferocious and complete, tested
names like they were your first garments. At night
I dreamt you were called *cool skin, smooth rain*.
But for now, I embrace you nameless. You visitation,
you pure animal, you shocking creature, you moon-headed boy —

September 1996

March: Second Trimester

One crocus has opened an orange eye
in John's garden — we'll see how it likes
the frost; its sisters are still sleeping,
their bud-cases lucent green
between leaves. The unseen
unfolds. I parse the frightening lists
of the "Best-Odds Diet" and wonder best odds
on what? And think of all the cold
sudden last week, wonder if consciousness
will come with spring, the leaping of things
to their apogees. The world
under this one is poised,
wondrous. To think it
will clamour for water and light, for
mineral nutrient, the songs of sparrows,
steady warmth: that seems
nearly impossible now. As if a voice
has asked to be taken along somewhere
even though, this morning,
I leave the house alone.

What Moves

In their grey and black flashings, the smallest
particles cross atomic space pantherlike. A rush
to being. And beneath that motion (motored

by the same ions trapped
in a comb!) all is silence, the silence
of the spaces between things. That's

not much to go on. But enough
to wonder at how you filled this year
one microbillionth at a go,

blooming with the shape of us, two pictures
held up to the light. We worried
like all first parents waiting

while that roil of stars and darkness
coalesced to you, who arrived, surprisingly.
Grey, wet, sweating nutrient, quick

to suck. Math-loving atoms, clenched into *body*,
assumed alikeness, which delights. I now hold
this infinitesimal, that gathered its forces across

vast nothing in order to be called to life.

Offering

I was alone with you after everyone was gone
and life was in you like a charge in a wire. Your poor
head in my hand, musketball heavy, your eyes roving
for purchase in the blue and grey room. They had you
in a tiny surplice, not knowing
they didn't have to make you look holy, you were
already ministering to me.

The world you came from was already fading, a cry
from another room. This one so rude to want
so much of you already. Who wouldn't cry for it
in your position? Instead, serene, you somehow
manage peaceful silence, saving up for the yaw
of life, its raw colour and noise. Carrying you in
through the garden, you seemed to fit between the rain.

When you open your mouth now, there's a pink
quiet there, a cradle for speaking to grow in. It pulses
sound inchoate. But no words
are needed yet, no names for things,
no answers, no prayers, despite your head,

which nods in supplication, your white
choirboy hospital gown. For now,
you are the only word and the mouths
of our bodies spoke it.

Whole

Days away from the winter solstice it's late earlier
and even darker at ten than I remember those blue streets
under my window when I was a child. Then, you could hear the cars
with their frost-steamed red headlights pulling out over gravel
from the temple lot. Behind us, the ravine was choked off
in all those back gardens, the parched rosebushes, fuscia,
the transplanted fruit trees pulling water from the willows.
Now, late at night, my own family is sleeping, you and your mother
recklessly asleep, arms splayed apart, your mouth flushed and red
and damp as the amaryllis down here, still clenched in its shivering bud.
I used to be afraid of this time of night, its stillness and its turning away
in silence from the living, and in fear, I'd go sleep between my own
parents. And yesterday, they placed you against me
on the gurney, to feed you so you'd keep still. You drank, staring
at me while behind you your heart moved on the echo screen
in three dimensions. This might be the last time it gives up its secrets
this easily. Soon they'll tell us there's nothing to worry about,
as if a hole in anyone's heart could be nothing
to worry about. That's not a true thing to me. It's a distant fear,
a possibility, like these blueing streets beneath these windows
that seem to me now to be the other ones as well, from
another part of the city, another part of my life.

Marriage

When it rains, there is a nearby sound, its multiple
onenesses, the circles that are closed
as soon as you hear them, the spatter in the flowers, the leaping-up
on the shiny railings outside the window. And there is
a far-away sound as well, a singleness, movement
in the distant air, over the lake, beyond the farthest trees,
a sound that is probably the rest of the world.

Star

Is he sleeping? — our midnight
mantra, one of us walking
all stealth into the room. A ribbon
of streetlight drapes pale blue
like a wreath and his head,
deaf to its body, flops away
from brightness. The dog
is carefully unamused, scatters
under the bed. We hear the soft grunts
from the bassinet, soon he'll cry
and we'll have our newest discussion,
should he sleep with us, is it bad for him,
will he be scarred if left alone?
It seems a pointless
disagreement, like thinking
you could spoil the stars
just by looking at them. Then
he cries harder, his two-cent lungful,
and the question's gone, you lean down and lift him out
and once between us he subsides, a cloud
that passed over the moon. *Is he asleep*, you'll ask,
and then silence, the answer flooding in.

Night Swimmers

Our bodies, exhausted from the heatwave drive,
    hang like drops of batter in the lake.
        Scars of pale white under water, vellum
           moving toward islands. Meanwhile,

   he's sleeping in his green pyjamas in the cabin. Long past midnight,
      a covey of barn swallows
        will burst up from the eaves when we go in. Now,

        our bodies glow white in the lake — memory's
           a pale bloom in the deep blueness of everything else forgotten —

        stories heard in the night, shapes moving toward islands.

Alembic

At eight months, the hard work of distillation is nearly complete.
From the strange bones of my men, the old flesh of your women
comes this struggling animal, this boy. Learning
to stand, he rises over your side of the bed, a living pun, and you both laugh.
His body a language straining to become the one we speak in our world,
although he really wants to return *you*
to some safe place inside himself. This is animal love, the way
he watches us hugging, turns his wolf's eyes to me, saying *so,*
how do you think this is going to turn out? He's mostly
what I want to say to you now, the best version of myself.
He carries to you the halfmoon of my bottom lip, the hint
of a great-grandfather's red hair — alembic and alchemy:
newly beautiful things. Gifts from the shattered world of men.

Green Famine

It's Lyle's phrase from the back of the car, Danny telling him, Dad
I told you if you were comin along you keep your gob shut, then swerving
to pass a truck, the rain-slicked road shimmying underneath: some
kinds of love it's taking me years to understand. Anyway, says Lyle,
this kind of rain comes too late to save the orchards, the trees
are green, but you can't eat the fruit. Earlier, counting hours, I'd watched
the plane's shadow cover a lake like a hand over a mouth, then the silvered
towns clustering where roads met. Whorls of grey rock there, like something
stirred into stillness, motionless in green. The rain blackened the highway
and we came off fast into New Glasgow, the bag of apples sliding across the dash.
Those came from away, Lyle bitches, some other garden where the seasons
are working, but Danny ignores him, leans across. Take a couple, he says,
she'll be hungry, and I do, but I eat them both myself, grieved
by their fullness, in the hospital parking lot.

August–September 1999

The Ball

The river in Letchworth Park
was missing. We stood on a blank cliff, looking down.
Logs lay there like splinters in a finger, iron filings
blind to North. We walked up a hill to a barn, counted
seven doors bricked in, an unwillingness, over time,
to enter a space the same way. The windows were black
with grime, we could only imagine
what work must have gone on in there. Maybe the river
was inside, trapped in the dark, put to some
unthinkable task, such as milling light. Later,
I saw your arm running south by southwest beside me
in the bed, your fingers
closing around an invisible ball.

August 1997

Nuclear Family

Here we are, the family of the future, you baking pies, me reading books.
The baby covered in a blue shawl sits in the rocking chair, a tiny old man

watching the cartoons. He points and grunts, howls in rapture
if something on four legs goes past. *Goggie!* he shouts at a horse. *Goggie!*

he shrieks at a cow. I want to say, *Those aren't dogs, you dummy*, but I don't
because he's only a year and a half, and I want to be

The Good Father. Soon you walk in with fresh pie and say *how are my boys*
and we both smile at you. To think, this is the new life. Pie and love

and babies, and I used to be afraid of something, only
I don't remember what. You cut us both slices. *Goggie!*

says the baby. We eat in happy silence, the television
flaring silently in the corner, the child smiling at you

ceaselessly. I think I had been afraid of the future, believing
it wouldn't speak my language. Now I know

it hardly speaks at all.

First Birthday

All night long we ate your cake for sustenance, the dog's
yellow eyes burning over you in the cabin, her long black body
a primitive vigilance. After you were born, the pale nurses
swept in like ghosts and ministered to you while the machines
kept count of your existence. You frightened us, deciding maybe
to turn back, and you went grey and washed out by daylight, hanging
in a nest of tubing like a hollow egg. I walked down into the old halls
with their windowless doors where the long-dead children
lingered, claimed by the things now simple to cure.
Then they released you to us and we swept you home, locked
the doors. Monstrous to prepare like that, for all of life
to unhand us suddenly, an actuarial moment, something drawn back
to reveal where we fit. But we evaded it; you lived, we spent
a summer morning decorating your first cake and at night danced
as though grief had never threatened us. Sugared from the day and safe
you slept beside the dog who knew how to carry live animals
in her mouth. She slipped like a dark oil into the night when we came in,
and lay in the grass and we lay near you and breathed your air
and by morning we'd all moved through each other, like blood.

September 1999

Second Birthday

Do not rub antiphlogistics on tender areas just because they hurt.
Keep your fingers out of the rear ends of animals. Do not move a dead dog
off the road in the middle of traffic. This last is non-
negotiable. Your uncle and I learned the hard way: the huge black
newf in the road we found on our way to York Mills Arena,
our skates around our necks. Griefstruck, we stopped.
Mark directed traffic, his Stan Mikita stick in the air over his tiny body,
cars cresting the hill below Harrison Road. I bulldozed it to the side as the
95A banked around me to pass, the swish of it on the hardpack,
riders looking down from orange windows. Then our father
arriving in the '77 Lincoln, parking sideways, eyes glassy with fear,
your uncle keening in the dusky road for the dead thing. Heroism, we thought,
and there might be a thousand wrong beliefs at a time like that.

No one knows the flash points of daily life. The sudden calamity
of a head against a stone (the shallow dive, tug-of-war in the garden,
an innocent step backwards off the landing), nor the turnings in the course
of pleasurable things. Choking death from eating Pop Rocks with cream soda
(it claimed Mikey, the cereal-commercial boy), peanut butter, lollipop sticks,
the baby tottering into the midst of laughing adults, his mouth

foaming with kitchen poison, falling, goggling his keepers.
How to stem these lethal imaginings, what fears
to arm you with? The water from your sea monkeys
is not for drinking! Do not staple yourself!
Leave the mushrooms in the grass!

Imparfait

A continuing action in the past — you were sleeping, your
dark hair lay across your neck. I was waiting for you
to wake. The sensual returns in a shock of recall, always
a few gestures repeating themselves — looking off
behind the window in the door, waiting for someone,
laughing, hands flat on the table. Or the baby, balancing on one knee,
fingers spread out like he's waiting for someone
to roll a piano into place. These things are lying in wait
for old memory to claim them, scrubby blurred film reel,
scratchy recall of a voice or music *from then*. Everything
seems to be happening now all at once: *simultaneous actions
in the past. Description of a state.* While I was loving I was loved.

June 1999

Stadia

(3. also, stage or period of development . . . *OED*)

Exhibition gone now, my snow-clenched childhood there,
later it was a frayed basket for old balladeers. Good citizens, we sat
scoring apocrypha into programs with cold pencils, my father's
earphones buzzing with the story of the game below. Some day
I'll take you to where it began, we'll drag your mother too,
see the long flies leaping out of Wrigley, the busted street signs, the park
bright in its neighbourhood of trees. Happy for all escapes:
this strange green and white, still-then-dashing life. The snow
spun past the opening pitches that April,
I watched on the TV in your grandparents' bedroom,
the hard hollow cold beside Lake Ontario.

You will have this wholly bearable life. Like me, you'll
inscribe the shorthand of a balk or infield fly, memorize
the names of men who'll later be forgotten (by all
but a few grown-up kids), their faces turned up
to the lights as the anthems make your cheeks prickle even though

you don't want them to. I think of my father in sudden fits of delight,
leaping up with the crowd, the animal of the crowd. Will you feel,
as I did for him, this pleasure of silent connection? This night-game
late-inning last-up surge of love?

September 1992 and November 2000

Lac Brome

In the snowcovered townships, villages like strung beads
flash up and fade under the black sky. Back home, the poinsettias
are beginning to pale, the wreckage of a season turning to memory:
the songs, the table groaning under the best china, the children
calling down from their beds. All of it distant now as we drive through the town,
its yellow fourways blinking. I've forgotten the silence of these shortest days,
how coming home from school it was already too dark to go out again,
passing the families in their windows, bent over their plates. There's only
a few minutes left of childhood, its fragrance. Skating down at York Mills,
we'd pass the hedges beside the big houses heavy with snow, the white icicle lights
up until New Year's. By March, a path worn in from the road to the school.

Fighting

from the long car trip, the baby sweating in his carseat behind us, we drive the road
that clings to the lake. Carried on from one place to another these days,
like being borne on a wave, its rhythms. Out there, on foot, someone crosses
the frozen lake, a flashlight weaving in the darkness. Soon we'll pull in,
start a fire, cradle the limp baby down into bed, cover him. Animals
without number are invisible in the forests nearby, gripped by winter, in
sanctuary. Many hours later, the fire down to orange ember, I'm thinking about
the person we saw on the lake, that feeble light seeing her somewhere. Was she
leaving home? Was she going home? Another thing to go on with,
not knowing.

Premonition

The house is near a forest.
The rooms are pinwheels of light.
Many generations have passed.
There is a worn rattan chair in an attic.
Someone has been named, accidentally, for a killer.
The languages have merged. A poem
is consulted for signs a hundred years
after it was written. Tomorrow
you will remember something
that never happened.

A Table

Broken down in moves between houses, the crenellated green
board-top tucked flush against a van-wall, the four numbered legs
to be set up in one order only in the light of a new kitchen. Dinners
there with people loved or longed-for, the plates afterwards,
the candles guttering. For years, it had a glass top and underneath
stills from films, a picture of Vanessa Bell's dining-room table
painted appealingly yellow and green. Now,
rarely used, it sits in a gap of silence, burdened with books
and plants, life-trailings. I see it under a window in 1985,
overwhelming a tiny white kitchen with a park outside,
and beyond the park a street. I follow the street in my mind
and it slips into another one. Deft illusions of the
remembered world, difficult to reassemble. For now,
moving again, this twenty-year table will do. We'll get
something new when we're all older, call that one
the dining-room table for a while, then send it down its cascade
of guises, to be passed on, tucked away, its parcel of stories
among basement boxes. I take the old one apart, pile it
in a jumble against the wall, this beloved thing
that says *home*.

The Rooms

Wallpaper pasted up years ago comes off easily, a trowel unfurls
thin pale sheets of it. Behind: the long-unsunned white walls
raised by the young couple whose name we found in the city register.
The new mother stood here, head tilted, imagining the future's pattern
as a bright repeat, and in our new rooms she lay her children in their beds,
opened curtains on a wash of light — days and nights like this, a good portion.
The boys saw the trees leaf in spring from the windows — her father
planted it and the others, a housewarming gift to them all but now
the trees reach over the roof, will have to be cut back, a job
for one of our own springs. We find her X behind a medicine cabinet, a mark
where she wanted her husband to hang a mirror. Down years of standing
before it (on a box, then without) the children watched their faces change.
And in the middle bedroom you discover floral wallpaper in a closet,
this woman who wanted flowers, even in the dark.

We won't know her, not by these hints of living we erase
as we go through, making the house our own. The old carpets
are going, the walls will be shorn to white again, shivering in the biting air
before, heads tilted, we decide on colours. Our one boy, his brother on the way,
runs through the house with someone's hammer, ramming the last of the ghosts
through the floors. And so, that other family is gone. Our lives will take up

where theirs have stopped, our new marks fresh for now, even though we'll eat
in the same rooms, make love in the same rooms, sleep in them too, as if
slipping along in channels worn by that mother, that father. And we'll wake as well
in the late silences, to walk the halls among all the parents and watch the children
in their beds, grateful for the bright repeat of nights and days, the shadows
falling across their bodies from trees planted by another's beloved dead.

Farewell

No poems after midnight now, no more heartless poems of black-
hearted youth, spent and angry, the entire physical world
bent to their purpose like spells cast in a petri dish.
Now blue quiet spring streets outside, you and the snuffling child
rattled to sleep by a wet chest and the humidifier
soughing in the corner. So long to all those 2:00 AMS
with their parenthetical hopes (granted, mostly sexual)
yours dense with armies of beloved *beaux*, mine
stacked with bone-stupid striving, unhappiness
nursed. No minor miracle this, arriving out of the storm
merely fat and weak-backed, but loved and lucky, no tattoos even
of the forgotten versions. Strange blessings to cripple the past with;
so long, cold ogre, goodbye, goodnight.

Acknowledgements

These poems were written between 1988 and 2001, and many predate earlier published collections. I've tried to preserve a rough chronology in the structure of this book, to reflect the build and development of its various threads. Where, for the sake of establishing other tensions in the structure I've moved a poem well out of order, I've inserted the approximate date of composition at the bottom.

These poems were written mainly in and around Toronto. Some of them have already appeared in print. My thanks to *The Malahat Review, Arc, Vintage 97/98,* and *This Magazine* for publishing them. My thanks as well to the Ontario Arts Council, the Canada Council for the Arts, and the Toronto Arts Council for support during various periods when these poems were written.

To Don McKay, who lent his excellent ear to this book and found many places for betterment, my friendship and gratitude. My thanks also to Martha Sharpe and Adrienne Leahey at House of Anansi for guiding the book through the press, and to Angel Guerra for the beautiful cover. Finally, to Anne, Benjamin, and Maxime, who risk living with a poet, much more love than I can say.

MR
January 2001